THIS BULLET GRID JOURNAL BELONGS TO:

_____

CREATIVE NOTEBOOKS

We would love to hear from you! Connect with us at:

✉ info@creativenotebooks.com

➤ www.creativenotebooks.com

⽫ facebook.com/creativenotebooks

⊡ instagram.com/creative.notebooks

SOME SIMPLE LAYOUTS
to get you started

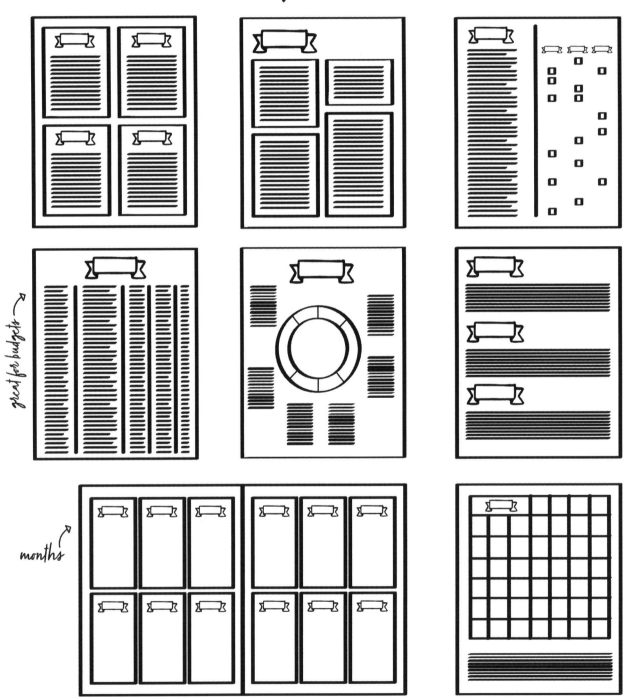

great for budgets

months

A LITTLE ADDITIONAL
inspiration

- BUDGETS/FINANCIALS
- GROCERY LISTS
- MEAL PLANNING
- FITNESS LOG
- WEEKLY CHORES
- COURSE PLANNING
- SELF CARE
- APPOINTMENTS
- HOLIDAY SHOPPING LIST
- BOOKS TO READ
- IMPORTANT DATES
- BIRTHDAYS
- SLEEP TRACKING
- WATER TRACKING
- DEADLINES
- RECIPES
- ACCOMPLISHMENTS

- DOODLING
- EXAMS
- GOALS & DREAMS
- CALENDAR
- MEDICINE
- HABIT TRACKING
- DAILY TO-DO LISTS
- DIARY WRITING
- MEMORIES
- STORYWRITING
- BOOKS TO READ
- TRAVEL PLANS
- SONG LISTS
- SCRAPBOOKING
- PARTY PLANNING
- BUCKET LIST
- AND MUCH MORE!

CREATE YOUR

Key

...AND GO!

Made in the USA
Columbia, SC
12 July 2017